SECRET**W**EAPON

SECRET**W**EAPON
Selected Late Poems

BY
Eugen Jebeleanu

Translated from the Romanian
by Matthew Zapruder and Radu Ioanid

COFFEE HOUSE PRESS
MINNEAPOLIS

Coffee House Press books are available to the trade through our primary distributor, Consortium Book Sales & Distribution, www.cbsd.com or (800) 283-3572. For personal orders, catalogs, or other information, write to: Coffee House Press, 27 North Fourth Street, Suite 400, Minneapolis, MN 55401.

Coffee House Press is a nonprofit literary publishing house. Support from private foundations, corporate giving programs, government programs, and generous individuals helps make the publication of our books possible. We gratefully acknowledge their support in detail in the back of this book.

Good books are brewing at coffeehousepress.org

LIBRARY OF CONGRESS CATALOGING-IN-PUBLICATION DATA
Jebeleanu, Eugen.
[Poems. English Selections.]
Secret weapon : selected late poems / by Eugen Jebeleanu ;
translated by Radu Ioanid and Matthew Zapruder.
p. cm.
ISBN-13: 978-1-56689-206-3 (alk. paper)
ISBN-10: 1-56689-206-6 (alk. paper)
I. Ioanid, Radu. II. Zapruder, Matthew, 1967– III. Title.
PC839.J4A2 2007
859'.134—DC22
2007021124

FIRST EDITION | FIRST PRINTING
1 3 5 7 9 8 6 4 2
Printed in the United States

ACKNOWLEDGMENTS
The translators would like to thank the Editors of the following publications, where many of these translations first appeared: *Circumference, Exquisite Corpse, 811 Books, Fence, 14 Hills, International Poetry Review, Jubilat, Meanjin, Painted Bride Quarterly, Parthenon West Review, Radical Society, Salt Hill, St. Petersburg Review, Slope*, and *Verse.*

The translators would also like to extend our great gratitude to the following people, who supported us in various and essential ways with the making and publication of these translations: Andrei Codrescu, Maria Bucur, Mircea Munteanu, Anneli Ute Gabanyi, Adam Sorkin, Brian Henry, Joshua Beckman, Peter Richards, Srikanth Reddy, Christopher Mattison, Dara Wier, Travis Nichols, Ioana Ieronim, and particularly Alexandra Zapruder, Florica Vieru, and Tudor Jebeleanu.

Special thanks to Horia-Roman Patapievici, Mircea Mihaes and the Romanian Cultural Institute, Bucharest for their generous financial support of the publication of this book.

CONTENTS

INTRODUCTION

EUGEN JEBELEANU: THE EPIC PROJECT & THE MELTED UTOPIA

Andrei Codrescu

Allen Ginsberg worked for years on a mammoth anthology of "epic poems" from around the world. To Allen, the epic poet was a socially engaged bard on the model of William Blake, Walt Whitman, and himself. Such poets took on the polis by its radical roots and shook it with prophecy, curse, and chant. Their purpose was to restore or to affirm paradise on earth, to take the kingdom back from the molochs. To this purpose they were willing to sing until their voices gave out. The early and mid-twentieth century was not deficient in epic poets. In Russia there was Mayakovski, whose mid-century heirs, Yevtushenko and Voznesensky, sounded the first notes on the trumpet that eventually brought down the Berlin Wall. In Chile there was Pablo Neruda. In Turkey there was Nazim Hikmet. In Greece there was Yannis Ritsos. The paradise these poets allowed themselves to be seduced by was not kind to them. Mayakovski committed suicide when the utopia was highjacked by Stalin. Neruda flirted with Stalin and lost his epic power. Hikmet and Ritsos spent long years in fascist prisons. Yevtushenko and Vosnesensky became historical after their "liberal" patrons in the Communist Party ended up in the garbage heap of history. These poets had aligned their access to cosmic forces far too close to the temporal powers, a mistake neither Blake nor Whitman nor Ginsberg himself ever committed. And then, what of the "epic poets" who cared nothing for the present stage, poets like Saint John-Perse, who identified with the ocean, or Lautréamont, whose sense of the ridiculous was entirely too elevated for bourgeois panegyric? The truth of the matter is that Allen wanted to make an anthology of poets like himself, in the touching belief that every nation possessed an Allen Ginsberg. Not every nation has a Ginsberg for two reasons: not every nation is the United States and secondly, in the century just elapsed, Ginsbergs were savagely suppressed unless they started praising management.

Romania's epic poet is Eugen Jebeleanu. At first, Jebeleanu was an epic poet whose soaring lyric achieved an apogee of engagement in "The Smile of Hiroshima" (1959). This poem documented so vividly the cries of the evaporating children of Hiroshima, we cried in our Cold War classrooms and swore to fight for peace. "The Smile of Hiroshima" was of a vintage with Picasso's dove, and represented the apex of Soviet efforts to paint itself as the good guy. Clearly, Jebeleanu believed the promises of the Soviet utopia. The myriad ghosts of the postwar world drank hopeful verse like water. Jebeleanu rose in the ranks of Party management, aided by a stroke of luck in cultivating a young Ceausescu, future dictator. Like Neruda, Jebeleanu garnered the commie literary prizes, and was Nobel material. Yannis Ritsos, fellow epicist and utopist, took refuge in Romania. At a certain point in the late fifties, Romania was like a seaside resort for faithful socialist-realists. Very few of the native bards who mushroomed in the literary congresses, pickled in vodka, had any talent. A series of pseudonymous nonentities like Ion Brad (pine-tree), marched side by side with the convinced Jebeleanu, the (perhaps) sincere Mihai Beniuc (former avant-gardist), and the euphonious Nina Cassian (former and future avant-gardist). The Party loved them all. Until things fell apart. All things, but the utopia first of all. The Communist party became nationalist, the international epic voice was muted in favor of folk kitsch. The expressionist fascist poets who had been marginalized by the Stalinists came pouring out of the wings, pan-pipes in hand and flugelhorns dragging behind them. Jebeleanu woke up.

From the cocoon of shattered convictions and the dregs of epic utopia, Jebeleanu phoenixed out in existential protest lyric and disturbing dark music. He felt profoundly betrayed by his comrades, but not by his poetic knowledge. He felt punished, cast down, but protected by the poet's eternal allies: nature and love. In the short lyrics, birds (predatory sometimes), rivers, flames, the Ursa Major, the body and its secretions, shells, and animals (domestic and savage), provide the elements of a discourse on the passing of time, disappointment, and compassion for the weak.

These translations, splendid works in English, do the best they can, given the depth of allusion to a past that will never stop bleeding. If you had to be there (and are lucky not to), it's better that Jebeleanu render the experience. That the title of this collection is *Secret Weapon* testifies to the continuity of a militant heart in a body bent by facts. The "secret weapon" is, of course, poetry itself, stripped of its need to grin or to shout no matter what. The early Jebeleanu would have been home in Allen Ginsberg's anthology, but the latter one would have been closer to the cosmos Allen believed in.

Ginsberg never completed his grand project because, realistically, it couldn't be done. He might have collected two volumes: one for the poet on stage, engaged and utopic, and another for the poet off stage, being hauled away by the ushers for a beating by the deus ex machina. Jebeleanu would have been perfect for this two-volume Janus. We have here, in translation, his contribution to the second volume: the elegy of the apology.

TRANSLATOR'S FOREWORD

Matthew Zapruder

Eugen Jebeleanu (1911-1991) is one of Romania's best-known poets and public figures. From 1930 to 1980 he published over twelve collections of poetry, and won several of Europe's most important poetry prizes, among them the Italian Taormina and the Austrian Herder. He was nominated by the Romanian Academy for the Nobel Prize, and befriended some of the world's best-known leftist poets, including Pablo Neruda, Rafael Alberti, Salvatore Quasimodo, Yannis Ritsos, and others. A justly celebrated and idiosyncratic poet, Jebeleanu remains virtually unknown in the West. *Secret Weapon* is the first appearance of his work in English translation.

Born in Campina, Romania in 1911, Jebeleanu worked as a journalist, and began his career as a published poet in the 1930s. His literary career spans decades of great economic and political hardship and upheaval for Romania: the years leading up to World War II, the rule of the fascist and nationalistic Iron Guard, the postwar Stalinist Communist regime, and finally the corrupt and brutal rule of Nicolae Ceausescu, which lasted from 1965-1989.

Throughout his life Jebeleanu's behavior was often oppositional, though not systematically so. When confronted with what he saw as abusive behavior on the part of the authorities, he often responded by lashing out in impassioned anger that could be almost willfully careless. While courageous, his was not the analytical resistance of dissidents such as Vaclav Havel. His highly personal stance of protest revealed itself sporadically in life, and in its purest and most direct form in his poems, which oscillate among strong expressions of anger, irony, self-criticism, nihilism, and joy.

In 1936, early in his career as a journalist, and during a time of great political ferment leading up to World War II, Jebeleanu was sent by his editors to Brasov to cover the trial of a group of Communist activists. Among them was the young Nicolae Ceausescu, who had been beaten and jailed. Impressed by Ceausescu's defiance, Jebeleanu wrote a provocative editorial expressing sympathy for his fate. The effect of this act—coura-geous, risky, and typical of Jebeleanu—would several decades later influence the course of Jebeleanu's life in ways he could not at the time have possibly predicted.

After World War II (during which Romania fought first with the Axis, and then after a coup in 1944 under Red Army com-mand against the Germans), Romania fell under the control of the Communist party. Like many artists and citizens, Jebeleanu was for a time a true believer in the values and goals of Communism. In 1959 he published an epic poem, "The Smile of Hiroshima," an impassioned critique of the nuclear bombing of Japan by the United States at the end of the war. He would become famous for this poem in the 1960s not only in Romania but throughout Europe and Latin America.

Meanwhile, Nicolae Ceausescu continued to rise in the Romanian Communist party hierarchy, and became the leader of the country in 1965. Flattered when reminded of Jebeleanu's early defense of his behavior in the 1930s, and aware of

Jebeleanu's already considerable fame, Ceausescu gave Jebeleanu a government sinecure, as well as wide latitude in the publication of his work.

Jebeleanu took immediate advantage of this freedom to publish his seminal volume *Hannibal*. Then he began to write and publish new poems of an even more startling directness. Beginning in the mid-1970s, he began to serially publish on the front pages of the major newspaper *Contemporanul* the strange, direct, emotionally blasted poems that would eventually compose *Arma Secreta*.

While Jebeleanu's position was unusual, his ability to publish was not. In Ceausescu's Romania some writers who disagreed with the regime were allowed to publish, while others were brutally persecuted, silenced, or forced to emigrate. Ceausescu's political strategy toward intellectuals and artists was, for the most part, not to repress and imprison artists (and therefore create further opposition and martyrs), but either cleverly to allow them just enough freedom to publish censored versions of their work, or to force them into exile.

Although Jebeleanu would continue to write over the course of the next decade until his death, *Arma Secreta* (1980) would be his last complete collection. Jebeleanu died in 1991, less than two years after Ceausescu was deposed and executed, at the very beginning of Romania's new post-Communist era.

At times, the poems of *Arma Secreta* come dangerously close to outright subversion. "The Fate"—which satirizes Ceausescu's wife Elena—was one of the poems published on the front page of *Contemporanul:*

She was so bowlegged
that Caligula on his horse
passed under her
with his whole army marching triumphantly.
Was she a woman? A witch?

Maybe a little of everything.
She had that traveling look—
and her forehead was a hearse.

Just as Nicolae was privately caricatured for his stuttering and diminutive size, Elena was mocked for being bowlegged. Everyone would have known exactly to whom this poem, with its sexual innuendo and insinuation that "she" is an embodiment of death, referred, and it was a great shock to see it published at all, much less on the front page of a widely-read newspaper.

It seemed even Jebeleanu's connections and fame would not protect him from the consequences of directly and publicly insulting Elena Ceausescu. Yet in the end, Ceausescu's cult of personality sealed him from this anomalous instance of public, if barely coded, criticism. No one wanted to be the one to tell Ceausescu his wife had just been mocked on the front page of the newspaper.

Yet the poems of *Arma Secreta* are not exclusively, or even primarily, coded acts of political resistance. They are clear, colloquial, and imagistic in both Romanian and English. They take place sometimes in a recognizable urban landscape, and at others in an animated natural world, where beasts, birds, stones, streams, potatoes, and trees all can speak. The voice in the poems, often harshly self-critical, continually expresses the pain and suffering of those around it. Often the speaker longs to see the dead again; sometimes he wants to merge with the natural world.

Not More

With a shout I resurrected silence.
From silence, I gave birth to the word.
A feather balanced in the sky,
a rabbit hid from the shout.
But I wasn't able to bring you back,
not even for a moment.

And all night the wind blew
a whistle in an endless tunnel.

The speaker understands the futility of speaking, yet feels compelled
to do so. He knows how hopeless it is to long for amelioration of
the great unnamed suffering he has brought upon himself, and
others. He considers himself pervasively guilty of unspoken
crimes against humans and the natural world.

A striking quality of these poems is the speaker's unwilling-
ness to set himself apart from everyone and everything, his refusal
to retreat into nihilism or self-justification. His resistance resides
not in his attempt to explain or justify or mitigate his behavior,
but in his need to expose his own responsibility for the unnamed
crimes that live on in their terrible consequences for the people
and things that surround him.

In "Brotherhood," the speaker pleads his case for an
unspecified crime in a pantheistic court:

It was a natural judgment.
I was sitting on a branch, and the crows judged me.
They said, Let him speak.

I croaked seven times, then again seven times,
three times secretly striking the bitter branch.
And they decided, He's right, it's enough—
and they tore me apart.

The crows aren't a different species from the speaker: they are brothers, the judgment "natural." Something deep is being exposed. The speaker, strangely, argues for his own punishment. He too is a crow, and his crow-like argument (croaking and striking the bitter branch) convinces his brothers to punish him, to tear him apart.

The famous verses by Pastor Martin Niemöller—an early supporter of Hitler who later courageously opposed the Nazis and survived the concentration camps—begin "When the Nazis came for the communists, / I remained silent; / I was not a communist," and continue in a similar vein (mentioning, depending on the version, trade unionists, the incurably sick, Jews, those in occupied countries, etc.) until its final couplet: "When they came for me, / there was no one left to speak out."

These words seem less a call to action than a sad acknowledgment of one of the great paradoxes of human nature. At the end of the poem, the speaker is taken away as a result of the failure to speak out and defend someone else who would then presumably defend him in turn. Yet if our motivation to speak out when others are abused and oppressed is merely self-interest and self-preservation, and not a moral objection, then we ourselves have adopted the mentality of oppressors, and are making the very calculation on which the rule of oppression depends. "They" expect "us" always to make a calculation of fear and self-interest, and trust and depend on the fact that we will never believe silence in the face of persecution and injustice is morally wrong on its own terms, and act accordingly.

Unflinching, clear-eyed awareness of the horrible paradox of
the self-preservation instinct—however understandable and
unavoidable—is what drives the late poems of Eugen Jebeleanu.
In them, the speaker feels he has failed himself and those around
him, by continuing to be alive while others perish and suffer. This
guilt and horror often externalizes itself in the form of horrible
monsters, such as the Chimera, who comes to visit the speaker in
the night, in dreams:

Chimera

A chimera is born from rain,
invisible rain.

Her hair is long,
and her face is on the back of her head.

The opaline tail of the chimera
arises from a horrible notion.
Ever since I was born
she has been hitting me with it.

Darkness and gray light.

Sometimes I try to get around the tail
to see the chimera's face.

Then the rain becomes stronger,
and I know something terrible shakes there
from rain and laughter.

Chimera is reading the news.

The voice speaks in the face of great mysteries and terrors, including the terror of knowing something is wrong, and not knowing how to resist. This poem, and this book, is the clear expression of the confusion and inability to articulate the "horrible notion" that exists as a consequence of being born.

The willingness to accept the consequences of this confusion and terror produces not polemics, apology, explanation, or historical remnants, but poetry. These poems continually reach toward the unspeakable and unspoken. In them, the speaker lashes again and again out in anger toward himself, for his complicity in the world that surrounds him and which he has played a part in creating.

In the middle of a very difficult and dangerous time, Jebeleanu spoke out, as clearly as possible and with a great self-implicating power and directness. These poems are what remains from his flawed, imperfect, human efforts. They reach out from their specific time to ours. Whether Jebeleanu can be called a dissident, a compromiser, or fellow traveler is a matter for his fellow citizens or historians to decide. For us, citizens of the richest and most powerful country in the world, those issues are, in the end, less important than the central spirit of these poems.

The voice in these poems speaks directly to us and our experience. Like the speaker, many of us surely benefit from our situations, and our situations depend on the suffering of others less fortunate than ourselves. We too are responsible for the inequities of our system, as well as the actions of our government at home and abroad. And surely many of us feel deep within ourselves a pervasive guilt—personal and civic—as well as a profound helpless confusion as to what we can do to change anything.

In 1996, when Radu Ioanid first read me a few extemporaneous translations from *Arma Secreta*, I immediately felt the direct language and dignified, dark energy of Eugen Jebeleanu's poems, and had the strong feeling these poems would be powerful and important in English translation. The voice in them clearly speaks to the people and world from a place of integrity, responsibility, and guilt that transcends any particular political situation.

These poems embody a spirit of resistance: not to the authorities, but to the self-justification within us that can distance us from each other. They are honest about the confusion in which we find ourselves in relation to our brothers and sisters. This need to once again feel a lost connection and responsibility within the poems is what makes them feel so contemporary. From the first time I heard these poems, they struck me not merely as historical artifacts, but as vital to human experience. And, sadly, in the intervening years they have only become more pertinent to our circumstances.

SECRET**W**EAPON

THE QUIET ONE

I dreamed I died, she said.
And she climbed up to me in bed, small and crying.
And danger shone black in her black eyes.
And I caressed her hair of light.
And I calmed her, telling her: It was just a dream.
She slept.

And she slept.

And I never dared to wake her again.

CHIMERA

A chimera is born from rain,
invisible rain.

Her hair is long,
and her face is on the back of her head.

The opaline tail of the chimera
arises from a horrible notion.
Ever since I was born
she has been hitting me with it.

Darkness and gray light.

Sometimes I try to get around the tail
to see the chimera's face.

Then the rain becomes stronger,
and I know something terrible shakes there
from rain and laughter.

Chimera is reading the news.

N I G H T

At night, lying in bed
on the narrow sheet, the sheet
riddled with senile wrinkles,
when my bones, my independent bones, are hurting me,
when I listen to the breathtaking songs of clang clang,
when I dream what cannot be,
when I memorize vaguely what was,
when I can no longer build
a coop for some problematic stars,
when what the Big Ones are preparing for us
over the ocean or in other places
no longer interests me,
when I can neither sleep
nor stay awake,
then
close to me
with large disgusting steps
with a body like a bored harpy
comes Lele,
great Lele,
Lele of Boredom,
Lele who without malice gives me
a slap on my ashen lips,
smothers my head in the rotten cabbage of the pillow,
and whistles bored through teeth that reach up to her ears,
"You have died enough. Now go on."

And I wake up tomorrow
in the lulling arms
of life.

SECRET WEAPON

This thing
so many despise
but everyone wants to make.
This thing
so many people
want to catch
so they dress up in the sirens of cars
which can go 100 miles per hour,
and in pressurized bottles,
and in dresses with patterns or with no rhyme or reason,
in dresses no less shiny
than neon on those evenings in summer
when I don't know who
high above us
is quietly
scything
the crops.
This despised thing
envied by all
because it cannot be seen
but exists,
because it is wolf and bird
and nation of lambs,
high, high where it rules
the moon
without saying a word.

This thing
so precious
it costs almost nothing,
which reveals itself to only a few,
giving itself to all,
wolf, bird, lamb
(without tail! without end!)
belonging to all
(if they can catch it)
which cannot be fashioned
by hands with flint finger bones.
This thing which sings,
which bites if it's needed,
which keeps you warm
wolf
bird
lamb
breath of the Invisible.

RECONCILIATION

Those who are gone surround us.

Such bracelets
of shining stones
surrounding a great treasure!

But what if the treasure isn't us,
but ones who live without any desire?

People, chickens and foxes, worms, and mysteries,
gold and iron, concrete and lead and silver,
and so many other metals, iron and chains and many
many cosmic riches . . .

Silent today, all immobile.

Do you want a palace?
If you want them, you can have them all.

But beautiful skull,
I can feel you smiling . . .

WITHOUT RESPITE

You are gone, but no matter what
I will not say,
"May she rest in peace."
Never.

May you not rest in peace.
Don't rest, be
waiting always.

Don't stay still.
Don't rest, my love,
don't rest, be
always in waiting.

And cursed be the one who says,
"May she rest in peace!"

Because he is the one
who tries to part us forever.

May not rest, but restlessness
pass through you
like one thousand points
of a star
and not give you rest
for even a moment
until I, too, arrive.

MIRRORED TEETH

How beautiful front teeth are!

These front teeth of mine
are not moving, no.
And neither is made
of platinum or gold.

My teeth are daisy petals
my beautiful front teeth
my teeth just like a teenager's teeth
my front teeth
(don't ask me about the others).

In the waters of the mirror
which do not lie
how beautiful front teeth are!

Unwavering.

And just by keeping them in my mouth
while in Pearl Harbor
Coventry and Vietnam
and in so many other scalding mirrors
Boom
went almost everything
I was able to save them.

Oh my lover
who doesn't appear in any mirror
I told you so many times
that a God still exists.

As long as there are still mirrors
and a few front teeth
left untouched to remind you
that not everything
can be destroyed.

OLD **A**CHILLES

Even if it seems that you're dead
you need to do everything
as if you were alive.

Let them believe that you still can fight.
Grow your snout longer,
in order to scare them.
Blow out your hollow cheeks.

And don't lie moaning in a sepulchral vault.
Lie moaning under a tent.

FLOWER AND BONES

The flower is air
and the air is a flower
and my bones hurt
because they want to fly

ON NEW ROADS

She sold things in the street
nobody bought
because they were made of paper.
Her shop was the air.
She was a sad bird.
It was I who made the things
a little smaller
than a handkerchief.

Mother . . .

EARS

I have two ears from which I can be pulled
by two people at most at one time pulling.
When I sleep I usually sleep on one.
The other is a candle.

But at any time I can be awoken
in order to report
why I am sleeping—or in order to be told
to sleep in order to report.

Come closer, but not like that other time
when a few hundred came.
Pinch my ear, but only one of them.
The other is burning.

M Y S I S T E R

This cow has such gentle eyes.
And she understands me better,
my brothers.

Because you no longer want me.
And because you would chase me off
much closer to death
than my friend, the cow.

She looks at me
with understanding eyes
made of light clouds and marguerites.

She is thinking about the slaughterhouse
prepared for her and for me
by that merciless, unseen force.

And her forehead is snow
and she doesn't wear glasses
and her temple is a moon
and she is guarding
but not stalking me.

TOOTHACHE

May the Big One not let you lose hope,
even when the small ones are losing
the weakened crossings and bridges
they don't even need anymore
because they carry nothing.
May the Big One transform
and may his wisdom teeth suffer an ache
and all that comes with it
so that even should he dream to possess
the crescent roll of the moon
may he not eat it,
may he not pluck it,
may he realize that this is refused
by wisdom teeth with their holes through which
the moon giggles and yellowly laughs.
And may every ha! of the moon
strike him with a pain
no one can cure.
Let the Big One give you
without being asked
all that he gives us:
a new Pain to awaken
you and allow you to join us.

THE SPRING OF ALL SEASONS

Now more than anything else
I believe in grass.
It gets paler during the night
in such a natural way
with transparent bees
that temporarily leave me.
Tomorrow they will tremble again
in their vestments made of sky.
And into the room you long ago abandoned
enters the chirping of meadowlarks pecking
the last scattered grapes of the stars.

My tired eyes, my heart of nineteen years . . .
Everything is possible.
And I passed, and I'm passing,
and I shall pass.
Forever I find myself in everything.
From my eyes I brush
the happiness of those who are gone,
happy that they remain in me.

I am a clearing.
I am full of the bluish flapping of sunrise,
cool going through me.
My forehead and lashes are frosted,
all the missing ones sing within me.
My blue lids are closing.
I will reawaken always.

AND I HAVE

What I wouldn't have wanted
and what I wouldn't have dreamed of
all that I wouldn't have wished
on any being.

Be happy and don't try
to understand.
If you wish
you can say I'm hermetic.

That I have closed myself
in a harp made of bars
emerging
from myself

and which I am
soundlessly shaking.

Having nothing to say
I say that it's good.

TOWN ON FIRE

Just before I would set it on fire,
I would yell, Get out of the houses!
But don't take anything with you!

And I would stay motionless—
shadow
and sign of light,
watching
how everyone would come out running,
dressed only in skins,
in their own skin.

Winged, they would leave
furniture the landscape of so many quarrels,
kitchens the site of so many shortages,
those same walls with their boredom
confronting
all those little shelves of books unread
for lack of time,
and time the color
of cold bread.

Now fly! I would shout,
blowing in order to lift them,
and they would fly, all of them,
without ever looking
over their shoulders.

INVISIBLE

Don't pay too much attention
when you follow me
The more attention you pay
the less you'll see

I am not where you think I am

I'm between spaces
I sing between sounds
I hide between bars
and not behind them

Stalked by a tiger
I'm safe not in a cage
but in the spaces between

Sometimes the moon
sneaks through

very pale

invisible

WHAT CAN BE DONE

I appeared in this world without volition.
I will remain as much as I can,
or am permitted, since I need so many visas,
for air and for freedom.

But in the end
I will become something that cannot be seen.
Something singing in water and smiling in stones.

CLARA
—for Joska M.

Oh, I see her hanging.
But she didn't hang herself.
That would have been better,
for she would have remained
just as beautiful:
noble apple
under a tree
cheeks so clean
so transparent
round flame of life.

Wherever she lowered her eyes
grass grew
potatoes communicated
amongst themselves
complicit, happy looks
wheat raised its eyebrows
even during a drought.

But she didn't hang herself.
Not from a tree branch,
nor from the question mark
of a hook.
She didn't hang herself.
She flew, she threw herself

from a balcony
toward the earth she made fertile.

She didn't want to remain in the air,
nor on the earth she loved.
She wanted not to be
anything any longer.
Neither apple, nor round flame,
nor nothing.
Nothing.
And she was guilty of nothing.

PATIENCE

No, the dead aren't getting bored.
Far away they are waiting for me to reach them.
And waiting, they leaf through a book
with wet pages—and they smile at me.

MY DOGS

I remember my lost dogs
especially at night.
One had fur like white tousled peonies.
Another had no fur,
he was born without fur,
and he trembled,
looking at me with his violet eyes.
Another resembled a certain red-haired general.
I gave him his name and he accepted it.
Another jumped into my arms when I found him.
Then he laughed, then he cried a little.
And not a single one of them had a pedigree . . .

The garden has been deserted for a long time now.
But once in a while
I hear them barking at me
from far away,
from the moon.

NOT MORE

With a shout I resurrected silence.
From silence, I gave birth to the word.
A feather balanced in the sky,
a rabbit hid from the shout.
But I wasn't able to bring you back,
not even for a moment.

And all night the wind blew
a whistle in an endless tunnel.

RAKE

To be a rake . . .
a rake made of stronger iron,
carried by a thinking hand
at sunrise and toward evening
to slowly rake the earth
and discover
from whom I am made . . .

POTATO IN THE CLOUDS

It's best to always
have less and less.
Fewer days,
less and less tobacco.

Not to be sad at all,
and to feel light.
To have only a dandelion,
and for you to be a cloud.

And to look higher
than an arrogant ruler,
and to look down with pity,
smiling, "poor lives."

And not to think, and never to say
"ouch," nor "ow," nor "oof."
And to choose from among the big clouds
a small cloud made of a potato.

TIME

I would take you in my arms, but I am frightened.

You are silent and to capture life
you talk all the time
(you believe, you are one who believes)
and the day is gone.

And now
you must rest.

The words flew
forever lost
away toward their autumn.

One grape
from a bunch of grapes
silently
rolls through fingers

and the day is gone.

BUT HOW

But how do wolves sleep?
With difficulty.
With fur made of snow,
stretching their teeth
toward what cannot be seen.

Bristling, with a sharpened snout,
they stay and wait for prey.
And in their frozen eyes
balances
an orchard of useless bones

through which the wind sings.

WERE YOU TO BEAT ME

I wouldn't say a word.
I would laugh a laugh
that would stun you.
You would become a marble fountain.

And from the tears
dripping onto those lips
so round
I would drink you.

CONSTANZA

Constanza, city I know.
Constanza of contraband stars and forgotten musk.
Constanza kissed by salty wind.
Where I walk, where I once walked.
Where there are crosses,
slabs of moon,
and a defunct finger of a mosque.

An ah for you happy young sleepwalkers,
an oh and an ouch to the one who only remembers,
and another ouch for me

Eternal Sea, lioness of waves,
pass a tolerant hand
over my dried old eyes.
You are parting forever from me.
You are coming back always
for those not yet found.

D I D O

Immobile
you are more beautiful
than in life.

Sublime.
Death found you
a perfect rhyme.

If you could see yourself
you would not want
ever
to have lived.

THE WAITING

The rooster woke earlier, but in vain.
In vain the bear moved its paw
a little bit faster from the hole in the tree.
Dawn shook the red kerchiefs earlier,
and earlier the waters lifted the fog,
but in vain, in vain!

For I heard a lost voice saying,
Come on, don't be stubborn.
Everyone's in such a hurry,
not for your highness who's waiting,
but for the cloud of snowdrops
with a young smile . . .

LESSON

I have to learn how one dies
(because in living a man lives however he can)
from birds who disappear in song
from blue sky gliding into a rose
and from the river
without a care
which goes disappearing
over the coins of the fish

DIALECTICS

I learned from the water
how not to flow
I learned from the plow
how not to plow
and from life I learned
how to disappear

LEAVE IT BE

Leave those kerchiefs that you love,
purple, colorful, childish, blue.
They are all just meaningless banners.
I left them, and I love them too.
Their colors belong to times gone forever.
They don't blossom where the rosy embers burn,
nor in the definitive kiss of the eyes.
Look how morning flaps slowly,
whispering shirts, and multicolored blouses,
and pants torn from being worn
so often in rain and wind.
They have no flagpole,
and never hang at half-mast.
Let's listen to the story
of their eternal, ephemeral life.

HAPPY SAD

How is it I can write
something happy
about sad things?

You said yes:
handkerchiefs can hold
both smiling diamonds
and tears.

Oh, I know which is which.

Where is the handkerchief
that can cover a grave?

PRECARIOUS

This body of mine is like a worn-out shoe.
I whisper to myself, looks like it still holds.
And I pass through a forest lulled by rain.
And the rain passes through me.

BEFORE

How could I leave you?
Yet I will, oh I will without wanting to,
just as something much worse
pushed those animals in pairs
into Noah's monstrous ark.

I will move ahead without knowing
where or toward which road I go.
No star from silver and no star from lead
will come to my aid.

There will be smoke before and smoke after,
or maybe not even that.

And I will leave behind
some words in the snow,
wrinkles of sound
that without haste, calmly,
the wind will erase.

BATTLES

I hear the sounds of a beautiful performance.
Daggers battle, then come to life,
and men die.

There is a sidereal indifference in the eyes of my lover.
Ask what and where it happened.
The rest you can tell me some other time.

I pass a hand over my heart
through the shots they are firing
in order to calm her.

Far away weepy thoughts summon lightning,
then arrange themselves like snipers advancing
toward the potatoes which must emerge
tomorrow morning
with innocent newborn eyes.

But the bullets are falling harmlessly
from the barrels of the guns
without wounding anyone.

The wind has stopped.

At dawn the potatoes will retreat once again
into their angelic order . . .

HOW

How hungover old age is
especially when
the only thing which still smiles at you
is the lip of the grave . . .

You can almost say what it was
through two or three trembling words
when the sea sparks dew
under clouds building palaces

WINGS AND EARTH

A bird is a seed with wings
but the earth does not love her
she sprouts only by spreading her leaves
in skies plowed by the wind

DENII

At St. Nicholas church
we children blowing out candles
walking between tombstones
made happy by honeyflames
the soul of the hyacinths acknowledging us
oh happiness of Resurrection!
The compass of the falling stars
lulling us from the sky
And the laughing of teenage girls
where are they now?
And all who were and are no longer

And the chirping of those little birds
I don't die I don't die I don't die

THE MOST

Nobody could be
happier than me.

Because I endured so much,
and am still breathing
this green air.

The space in which I live
gets larger and larger.

Almost all my friends
have become blackbirds.
All I hear of them
is an occasional
flapping.

I don't care about anything
in this world full
of such weighty and guiltless
things.

Nobody could be happier
than me.

CRIB

She had sagging teats
yet her belly was full
and her laugh was naive
but also divine
like the gleam of Ursa Major.

And between her knees
lulled a wooden crib
heavy
as a moon.

Her face was ugly
but dignified
and she was always awake.

And she had small ears
like shells

Poor colossal nursemaid

FUTILITY

Oh how I prayed
I who am a pagan
for the poor girl who lived
only once and so hard
but died thousands of times.

Oh how I prayed
believing that I could reach
with my thoughts
the one who does not exist,
the one nailed to the sky with stars.

And I prayed,
not in churches to long saints
with spherical eyes,
but in my room
with its great halos of dust.

And Lord, it was all so futile.
Perhaps because I wasn't diligent.
Perhaps because I didn't know
how to launch enough prayers
for your voice
to listen to mine.

LATE

Everything must be done in time,
otherwise from far off you hear the bugle
send you the sound of a thorn
and you know it's winter.

SHARDS

Every day is a burden.
What once gave you pleasure hurts you,
what once was rising
now scratches the earth.
You want every day to pass
like some pain
and then to be done.
Sleep is a bag with its mouth tied.
A dream is what it was,
and cannot ever be.

Every child drops
like a tear which holds your reflection.
That reflection knows as well as you
how that child will become
just as you now are.

A sigh is a cloud without rain,
and without the scent
of the wheat through which you once walked.
You lift the years on your shoulders
and look around.
You are always more lonely.
Many fell without even reaching
that crossroads like a wheel
with three dented teeth.

And you are so broken
your weariness drifts
with no mooring.

Shards. You are thirsty
and don't want to drink.
And you cannot fly
and you cannot bury yourself
and near you glide shadows
which have lost their masters.

LET THE CAST IRON COME

Now let the cast iron come.
Let the slag come.
Let Himalayas of shrapnel
more disgusting
and more attractive
than the skin of a rhino
come.
Shrapnel which rained upon us
in the second
and in the first
and in all the wars which laughed in our faces
with the snouts of their guns
and the rays of their swords
and the infamous wheat of their slingshots
from the beginning
until now.
For at last we have reached the shiniest metals.
And now you can stop.
You who used others
to remove confusing gold
from the darkness of minds.
You who drew out
what was cleanest
until it filled with blood,
that sword which taught us
to recognize our eyes

blue
in the shining of bayonets.
Now let the cast iron come.
Cast iron which does not shine,
cast iron of stoves around which
we shall gather naked.
Iron cast without any glory,
iron cast like a black woman
hopelessly dying.
Let that metal which has never taken a single soul
into the earth or into the moon,
brother in metal to the skin of the rhino,
the cast iron metal,
come.

DE PROFUNDIS

Lay down your tears, go to the river,
and merge them with the tremor of ripples
forever reborn.

If you could tear out an eye and revive them,
would you do it? Yes.
But you know that I cannot.
Hateful creature, beast of Uselessness.
You mock my impotence.
You have punished us once again,
not for what we did,
but because with them
we feel most like ourselves.

Did you tear the little sparrow from us
because it didn't make
a vulture's shadow?
No. It was because it learned to chirp,
and was something you know
we would now miss.

The kerchief, the veronica—
here it is, balanced in the wind.
Little sparrow, sleep on the straw
made by rays of light.
You didn't know how to peck,

but only to sing.
Let the black and white keys of the ocean sing,
but very sadly,
let them even the sands of our uselessness.
Let the bells in the oaks rock,
sounding only in hearts,
remembering only your eternal faun,
Virgil . . .

And you who felt
cadences in a vacuum
made by one I met for the last time
in a timeless garden
where my blond harp still floats,
sleep there

where I will come soon.
Anatole! We will see each other
far from the beasts that creep on the earth,
far from those who despised us,
the unfortunate ones . . .
Because they are deaf
to the strange drums of the earth,
and to the sinister drum of the moon.

All of you passed the night quickly.
They never pass the night.
They shine.
You pass the night without even saying "good evening,"
even if a little ironically

54

you left us "on earth."
Into night. Night.

I am more and more cold.
I would shout but I have to be silent.
Maybe it's better.
All around there is so much noise.
I want a little piece of silence
and a little piece of earth.
Give me your hands, I'll blow in them,
and warm them with a few drops of dew.
Lift your hearts, my brothers!
We will see each other again.
The river is flowing quickly.
I am floating on its arms.

FRAGMENT

It was snowing hard.
You walked out onto that city's stone streets
holding a copy of *On New Roads*
in your frozen hands.

Because you were so small
you held the journal with care.
It was a butterfly
which could have flown off,
abducted by the anger of wind.

It was snowing hard.
You walked near the light of the stores.
It was warm there,
maybe there would be a buyer.

O, pity,
aged little girl with matches.
I followed you from afar
with so much shame . . .

You came out bent over.
Nothing.
The walls sustained you.
The big night was unfolding.
The blizzard frowned, reading the tiny pages.
And the angels of winter were trying to lift you with mercy.

FLOWERS OF SPRING

These flowers which appeared overnight
move and terrify me.
So sure of themselves,
so clean and strange . . .
They come toward me from everywhere.
They tear open, incarnating in themselves
everything white
and everything that is an echo
of innocence, the dream of hope.
Nothing can stop them.

I walk between them, staying away.
I walk between the moony bushes,
between sobbing trees
so white
between cherry trees with sleepy arms,
shining in their innocent shirts,
between so many signals
of an unending rebirth,
between the immaculate rustle of buds
wanting to explode.

It's an earthquake of flowers.

THE SADDEST

The saddest poem
is the poem which is not written
swallowed with knots
stalked by customs officials and bridges
the one which cannot be contemplated
not for anything ever.

Keep that poem.

She is surely the woman
who will give birth in pain.

And in her we shall each
recognize ourselves.

TOWARD THOSE LOST

We who want to go
toward those lost
can't be terrified by anything.

We give you everything.
Without any rhetoric
we leave it all behind.

We want to find ourselves again
by reaching those lost.

Here we are. They aren't . . .

Let's go on.

They must be further away.

MY LIFE

I'm looking for my lost life.
And I cannot find it.
My life is a bankruptcy.

And? And? And?

VENUS XX

Her teeth had all fallen out. She was still beautiful.
She had hips made of gulfs, and she swayed bluely.
She was entirely guiltless. She was walking straight ahead.
And she told me that she still had one more tooth.
She was so hot to the touch, so ardent.
I said, "At last a goddess who won't tell me lies!"

THE GOOD-HEARTED MAN

Being a good-hearted man
with a minimal salary
he died of a heart attack
grandiosely

STRANGER

This man is a stranger
but he didn't arrive with iron in flames
like you
my sweet brother

You whisper to me
you are the sun's watering can
your light is burning my eyes
so my tears fall

Not from happiness, as you tell him always
looking at me
wanting to see me forever dispersed
to him and to him and to him

Oh well so be it we have one life
take this finished one take it too
but I see that I'm not enough
that you have to burn everything

oh well, no

BROTHERHOOD

It was a natural judgment.
I was sitting on a branch, and the crows judged me.
They said, Let him speak.
I croaked seven times, then again seven times,
three times secretly striking the bitter branch.
And they decided, He's right, it's enough—
and they tore me apart.

THE CONFRONTATION

Then came seven lionesses
and they looked in my face.

O how my life lived in vain
was shoveled down my throat,
how my disgust began
to look through me harshly . . .

And far away only a bell, ringing . . .

THE TIP OF MY HEART

Let tears not fall from the trees,
unless I can gather them in my fists.

Whoever has ears
will see with the eyes
of the silent cat
who hunts without bells.

I cover the tip of my heart
but its beating gives me away.

Tears tumble
out of my fist
into the forest, a river of quiet.

HAPPINESS

Here I am with No More and No Less,
and with one more bag on my back.
After this you get a strong handshake,
the seal of nails in the arch of your palms,
and some drops wrung from geranium.

Their embraces are tearing the buttons
I myself sewed last night.
Mechanized lightning illumines my face.
Nadar has transformed me into eternity.
My wrinkles will all be retouched.

I went over there to the other side.
Congratulations.

CONFUSION

The moon is milkweed tonight
eaten by clouds with smoky beards.
My desire to go tears me apart,
but who can go with me?

The forest is a green immobile elephant
from which the trunk of the moon emerges.
Compare, compare without pause,
wise man who so resembles a fool.

BABY VULTURE
— for Tudor

Alert one
destined to climb
blue crests of mountains
through night and clouds
where the only arrows are herons . . .

Let him smile into his beard,
let him descend through clear air
down to sheep's wool clouds
leaving the earth's mute grass
to be grazed by oxen.

CLOTH

The cloth of the dead—so resistant.
And the dead themselves—so diaphanous,
such clouds traveling from what they were,
from the tombstone heavy with two thousand years.

Afterwards we will see,
and we will not see many things—
to see everything is to sing
always with nobody listening.

FABLE

I once knew a cow
who wasn't an ox, or a cow,
or even a calf.
It was a little bit of all of them.

It had the head of a chicken.
It laid small eggs of light.
It gave white milk like tiles,
without asking for a receipt.

It also had some defects.
It had no insects in its feathers,
and even worse
it laid its eggs without clucking.

Year after year it gave milk
and eggs without even a murmur
until the people shouted,
This must stop at once!

Why must it keep laying eggs?
A cow is a cow!
Let the harpy come
and transform her!

The harpy came at once
and sang.

And the creature perished.

THE FATE

She was so bowlegged
that Caligula on his horse
passed under her
with his whole army marching triumphantly.

Was she a woman? A witch?
Maybe a little of everything.
She had that traveling look—
and her forehead was a hearse.

UPSUR
—Babylonian monologue, 1093 BC

They don't let me say "oh"
and they don't let me shout "ah"
saying I have no choice
if I want to be anyone these days.

The same priests who said yesterday
I should launch my voice upward
say don't be scared today
and to slide downward on my belly.

I would growl or shout
but they say swim smoothly on sand
and when I want to sing a little—
I should make a violin from the earth.

WHAT STILL WAITS

What still waits for me
when death rings.
Only a death: mine, yours,
or maybe both.

And afterwards
let those who wish to stay warm
stay,
near the pale burning
of my former spark.

FLOWER DAY

It's so ugly all around me
that through the whole night
very beautiful ghosts
come to strangle me.

And still breathing I whisper
It's not enough, stronger,
stronger, because
it's Flower Day.

And the ghosts do not do
what I ask
nor what they want.
And they open their claws.

And whirling, they leave me
with their troubled wings.

ANNIVERSARY

Green as a fir
consumed for years
in hell's dark red crevices.
My friends are dead, armies disappeared . . .
Helmets are frozen echoes.

The celebration must be secret,
and only for the family.
Days don't have to hear about it,
because there are so few of them left.

Wait for visitors
so you don't sleep.

DON'T

No, don't enjoy
this life too much, this tumult
that makes you imagine
it's not the same thing as sand.
Don't imagine . . .
because it's like this.
From flames she makes ash.
From ash, wind.
And from what's made from wind
she makes a room without walls,
without words.

SO REMAIN

Don't ever ask anyone
anything. Don't ask
those who are sated, don't ask
those who don't have a crumb
because some have eaten
while others are hungry.
So remain, looking at the tables
just as you'd look at a sky
upon which two stars can be discerned
when the others understand
nothing at all.

METEOROLOGY

The snow I await
does not come

I don't want the hours
that come

January
and not a single snowflake

I softly turn

archangels of ashes
to snow

EGO

I'm caressing the fur
of an animal just out of the water,
like evening dew, or maybe
the kiss of dawn.
I need to feel my hand,
I need to caress,
to touch the creatures of the forest
in order to find out
something new
about me, the old one.
I would like to be under the earth,
but not dead,
to feel the fallen stars
hissing near me,
materialized,
(like corn popping in a fiery pan),
the sight of the onion, of thoughts
that blow after death,
the sight of the trembling crown
of the shout of a rooster.
I cannot not be.
When you will see me again
just as you believe,
it will not be this way.
You will not know,
I will appear in a different place,

I will have these faces
of the wind: fiery, cold, pale, brick.
I will disturb your absence,
but not from spite.
You will think sometimes of me.

PREMONITION

I will see you after I depart,
I will see you and you will feel me too.
I will look at you without hate,
and you will feel me
without seeing me
and your eyes will become a lake that trembles.
A long time ago a thread of a stone fell
into the lake, and you would like
to see it at least once more.
You will feel only pressing
absence upon your heart.

THE SAME

You can believe what you want about me.
Don't be tolerant.
I live like myself,
just like you,
and like you because of one death—
and despite the fact of another—
I will die.

FLOWERS AT THE STATUE OF EMINESCU

Why you would find this useful, nobody knows.
Meaning it isn't useful at all.
The poetry of poverty
is getting stronger everywhere.
The only strong ones
are those who can mount.
The horses get weaker and weaker,
and the horsemen more and more bestial.
And the ribs of the horses
are solar jewels
in the prison of dead visions.
And we deserve all these things
because we have earned them.
Now you are bronze,
and you don't care about anything.
Or, maybe, I don't know . . .
Because, last night
it seemed to me that
cautiously rotating
your infinite
oceanic
eyes
you pulled one carnation
from the wreath caressing your back
and swallowed it
secretly.

LATE GALLOP

An opaque brim of shadow
hung on my forehead.
Come on, I told myself,
you are a jockey
in the sky
of your late life.
You can still be useful,
even if you can no longer hold out
against the nurse with shiny steel teeth.
And I started to gallop,
between weeds, between forests, between
happy fawns with such tender, humid snouts,
between brilliant, fiery statues, until
I heard a voice whimper
It hurts, everything hurts.
And everything was hurting.
And I entered a cave without end.
And only the far-off snout of a deer
signaled me. And this is all.

AND STILL, ART

And still, Art chirps,
mute, deaf, unimportant,
without talking, saying
without hydras, without hydrates,
without nitrates, without urics,
without hurling, without howling
without laboratories,
without urinals, without millions and billions
and thousands of billions,
without battalions of miraculous investigations,
without relations,
without beakers, humid vines,
without electrolysis, without crisis,
without Parthenons of stupid knowledge,
without shiny windshields,
without colossal pyramids to build
in four thousand years,
without rats,
without poor, shabby souls,
and without poses
stands Art
with three roses
in her pale hand.

IN THE ATOMIC ERA

So many things have no scope
and some glow with such a pale sense
and the heart in its narrow shelter
trembles unknown
beneath the sky's immensity.

FROM WHERE YOU
DON'T EXPECT IT

From where you don't expect it,
jumps the rabbit, hop!
A sea rabbit,
a salt one, then one of pepper.

The sea gave me about forty thousand
white foam rabbits
somersaulting
filling the horizon with water lilies
and starring my sky.

One of them curled up into my arms.
From time to time
he smiles ironically,
and sometimes he emerges.
He is a gentle rabbit
of fiery snow

and he never wears epaulets.

SKETCH FOR A BALLET

A moon tries to disappear,
and sets the clouds on fire by gliding.
If I died tonight,
I wouldn't feel sorry at all.

Arm in arm two young people run.
They are two statues from the same play.
The earth remains.
O Brutus, O Cassius, O Italy . . .

EXACTLY SO

She thinks only about herself
and he thinks only about himself
and I think only about myself
and everything turns
around a ring
that holds all of us, saying
this is Life
this is the One
saying Humanity
is not a beast
but a lamb

COLD

I get cold in my jacket.
So I wrap it around me
more tightly.

My shirt is opening . . .
so I button it better.

The night comes.
It doesn't allow me
to think about stars.

The winter comes.
Be careful.
Cold is a shrapnel.

And what else . . .
Continue walking.

TRANSFER

The thoughts I began
had much rounder hips

Who asked you
to send them

On waves
of mute paper

But you don't ever have
to allow yourself ever

I don't ever
let myself ride

a horse of long coolness
through a forest

never walked
by anyone

TRANSFORMATIONS

Your braids once made curves of sunlight
on the hot belly of your mother.
Now long tresses of night
decapitated
from my skull by sleeplessness
will glide
until the day shows up
with those street sweepers made out of frost
that gather
fragments of memories.
Then the head looks for its shoulders
and doesn't find them.
You disappear silently
into the light,
thoughtfully braiding your tresses.

LADYBUG

A pale wind
has made me a ring
with a ladybug
for a diamond.

"Ladybug, ladybug,
wherever you fly,
that's where I'll
get married."

Who sang such a song
when I was a child?

Planes are passing, the day
passes, the night passes.

A red June bug
drowns
in the sinking moon.

Nightly
I look toward the ladybug
with her eyes
just like yours.

She looks back
with longing
and cannot fly.

BLACK SEA

Dolphins with their backs
like worlds of blue oil
can no longer be seen.
Everything changes—
and this is good.
The fabric of everything
always gets thinner.
Thus one can see
through an old, hand-held telescope,
the succession of time,
forever renewed.
Long life to Helios!
With his shiny hair
of gold dust and bone dust
from us and from others
who will surely pass.
Now a helicopter can land
on top of the minaret.
The last seagull leaves
with a wing dipped in oil,
a half crow
suddenly croaking,
and trying to hide
its remaining wing.

THE SOCIAL CONDITION

Not being a purebred dog
and not having a good name,
Krantz is kept on a dirty balcony
in the rain and wind . . .

HOW I DIED

Without any torment, without any torment,
only a weakness. And even that
was no longer mine, like
a few liquid branches
from a former oak
in a forgotten, faded, photograph.
One branch was summoned this way,
one summoned that way,
the others were all summoned other ways,
and the oak was now a sort of water,
a sort of sea of piano keys,
every key a transparent spade,
and every lip of water
indifferently murmuring
the spade, and the shovel.
And I overheard two leaves whispering
Look, father is dying.

ABOUT THE TRANSLATORS

Poet Matthew Zapruder is the author of *American Linden* (Tupelo Press) and *The Pajamaist* (Copper Canyon), winner of the 2007 William Carlos Williams award. He teaches in the MFA program in Creative Writing at the New School in New York City, as well as at the Juniper Summer Writing Institute at the University of Massachusetts in Amherst, and is an editor with Wave Books. He lives in New York City.

Born in Bucharest, Romania, Radu Ioanid is an historian based in Washington, DC. He is the author of several books on Romanian history and the Holocaust, including *Sword of the Archangel*, *The Holocaust in Romania*, and *The Ransom of the Jews: The Story of the Extraordinary Secret Bargain Between Romania and Israel*. He works as Director of the International Archival Programs Division at the U.S. Holocaust Memorial Museum.

COLOPHON

Secret Weapon was designed at Coffee House Press,
in the historic warehouse district of downtown Minneapolis.
The type is set in Caslon.

FUNDER ACKNOWLEDGMENTS

Coffee House Press is an independent nonprofit literary publisher. Our books are made possible through the generous support of grants and gifts from many foundations, corporate giving programs, state and federal support, and through donations from individuals who believe in the transformational power of literature. Coffee House Press receives general operating support from the Minnesota State Arts Board, through an appropriation by the Minnesota State Legislature and from the National Endowment for the Arts, and major general operating support from the McKnight Foundation, and from Target. Coffee House also receives support from: an anonymous donor; the Elmer and Eleanor Andersen Foundation; the Buuck Family Foundation; the Patrick and Aimee Butler Family Foundation; Stephen and Isabel Keating; Tom Rosen; Stu Wilson and Melissa Barker; the Lenfesty Family Foundation; Rebecca Rand; the lawfirm of Schwegman, Lundberg, and Woessner P.A.; the James R. Thorpe Foundation; the Woessner Freeman Family Foundation; the Wood-Rill Foundation; and many other generous individual donors.

This activity is made possible in part by a grant from the Minnesota State Arts Board, through an appropriation by the Minnesota State Legislature and a grant from the National Endowment for the Arts. MINNESOTA STATE ARTS BOARD

 TARGET.

To you and our many readers across the country,
we send our thanks for your continuing support.

Good books are brewing at coffeehousepress.org